Introduction

Amsterdam is a small city with a very big personality. Its picturesque canals, bordered with beautiful seventeenth-century houses and spanned by more than 1,200 bridges, lend it the air of a film set, and its people are renowned for their lively, open-minded and welcoming character.

The city has its origins in the late twelfth century, but it became a centre of the world's economy in the seventeenth, with the onset of the Golden Age. Huge wealth brought rapid development in every direction; this was stalled by recession in the early nineteenth century that was brought on by French occupation, but the Industrial Revolution put the city back on track.

In May 1940, the Germans invaded the country, and in the horror that was to follow, Amsterdam lost 10 per cent of its population. It took some years to recover, but from the 1960s the population grew and diversified, and the city became a draw for hippies, who cemented a free-spirited ethos.

The Hague may be the administrative capital of the Netherlands, but today Amsterdam is the country's largest city and its unequivocal commercial, creative and cultural capital. Its population of 780,000 is comprised of people of more than 170 nationalities, and this diverse mix has lent the city its reputation for tolerance and progressivism, which is part of the attraction for some 7 million international visitors per year.

Another major draw is Amsterdam's collection of more than seventy world-class museums, including the uniquely haunting

Anne Frank House, the Rijksmuseum, which recently underwent a stunning restoration, and the Van Gogh Museum, which has an extremely inclusive and accessible atmosphere (it's open late on Friday nights, with cocktails and DJs). Contemporary galleries are likewise constant sources of inspiration.

Be sure to check up-to-the-minute city listings before you book, as there are interesting events year-round, including art fairs, food and film festivals, a fashion week growing in stature, and, of course, King's Day, the national holiday that turns the city into an open-air party for the day.

Shopping in Amsterdam is a treat for design enthusiasts and for vintage treasure hunters alike. P.C. Hooftstraat, considered one of the best luxury retail streets in Europe, is home to the likes of Chanel, Cartier and Gucci; the Nine Streets of the Jordaan area is a picturesque district full of artistic indie boutiques, and there are a number of bustling markets to comb for interesting pieces.

While Amsterdam is famous for its 'coffeeshops' (where you can purchase and consume small amounts of cannabis), high-end coffee culture is also on a rapid ascent here; Amsterdammers are serious about coffee, and there are a number of world-class roasters at work throughout the city.

Stylish eateries are everywhere, and the chefs here have been successful in blending many influences into a distinctive restaurant scene, where snout-to-tail cooking, slow food and organic ingredients are all celebrated in chic environments. If you're

in the mood for something more casual, there are plenty of good-quality cool spots, as well as the vibrant markets, where you can sample Dutch specialities like sweet Stroopwafels, gooey Bitterballen, and fresh raw herring.

Amsterdam has a long-standing reputation for serving great beer in relaxed, understated brown cafés; in addition to this, it now has a thriving cocktail scene, with inventive concoctions to enjoy late into the night.

Amsterdam has attracted more than its fair share of controversy over the last number of years, due to prostitution (which is legal and licensed), tolerance towards the buying and consumption of cannabis, and the prevalence of rowdy stag and hen parties. But it is, in fact, one of the safest cities in the world; it has so much to offer that it is very easy to enjoy an exciting visit without encountering its edgier elements, if they're not your thing. All of Amsterdam's best attractions are within easy reach of the city centre on foot, and walking is the best way to stumble upon new and intriguing places, with which the city is overflowing.

With a confident, artistic, and friendly atmosphere, Amsterdam is a picture-perfect destination, rich with history and bursting with contemporary creativity.

Amsterdam is a wonderfully compact city, with most major sites in or around the city centre. It is also one of the best cities in the world in which to cycle. To get to destinations that are slightly further afield, public transport is straightforward, organised and convenient; the extensive public transport network connects the city's many districts by train, tram, metro, bus and ferry. Driving is strongly discouraged within the ring of the canals, and is very inconvenient due to the lack of parking spaces. Locals make use of an OV chipcard to get around, which is valid on all forms of transport, but for shorter stays, there are one-day, two-day and three-day Amsterdam Travel Tickets – again valid on all forms of transport operated by GVB – which make getting around easy and economical. These can be bought at Schiphol Airport (and are valid for the train journey into the city centre) and at numerous locations around the city. It is necessary to tag on and off each vehicle or station.

Getting around

From the airport

Travelling from Schiphol is a no-brainer, as there is a direct railway line to Amsterdam Central Station, with trains running every ten minutes. There are also shuttle buses that stop at many of the city's major hotels. Should you choose to take a taxi, journeys to most central locations should cost about €40.

Bicycle

Amsterdam is arguably the most cycle-friendly city in the world. Even though most of the sights are easy to get to on foot, we recommend renting a bike for at least part of your stay, as it's a way to experience the Dutch way of life (there are over 800,000 bicycles in Amsterdam) and a great way to see the city. Amsterdam is very flat, and with designated cycle paths it is remarkably easy to get around on a bicycle. There are a number of rental companies, such as MacBike, A-Bike Rental and Yellow Bike, where you can get a bike for about €8 a day. Follow their instructions on how to lock up your bike.

Tram
gvb.nl

The tram is the preferred mode of transport for many Amsterdammers. It is distinguished by its blue and white colours and you are sure to hear the famous bell that announces its presence to any pedestrians and cyclists getting in the way. The tram is one of the quickest ways to get into and around the city centre.

Bus
gvb.nl

Amsterdam's bus network is extensive, connecting the city centre with all surrounding neighbourhoods. Night buses are also available after the trams have stopped running.

Metro
gvb.nl

Amsterdam's metro system, which radiates from Central Station, is best used for reaching the city's outlying districts, such as Bijlmer, Amstelveen and Diemen.

Train
ns.nl

The superb train service provides connections with Schiphol Airport and other Dutch towns and cities, plus direct connections with cities in Belgium, France and Germany.

Ferry
gvb.nl

Amsterdam's ferries offer free connections across the River IJ for pedestrians and cyclists, and you rarely have to wait more than a few minutes to board. Get on behind Amsterdam Central Station.

Hotels

Conservatorium

The five-star Conservatorium, a sister hotel to London's Café Royal, is a
consistent presence on top luxury hotel lists, both in the Netherlands and
internationally. The neo-Gothic building was a bank, and then a music
conservatorium, before being transformed into a hotel by Piero Lissoni. It
has a breathtaking lobby lounge, two very fine eateries (an award-winning
Asian restaurant by Schilo van Coeverden and an all-day brasserie), and the
former drumming classroom now houses Tunes, a wonderful bar serving
over forty varieties of gin. There are 129 rooms (including 42 suites), all
featuring clean lines, muted neutral colours and dark wood, that range from
€300 to €1,000 per night. The hotel has the biggest spa in the country, and a
simply amazing concierge service. Offering the best in contemporary luxury,
the Conservatorium is, in its own words, 'beautifully composed'.

€€€€

—

Van Baerlestraat 27, 1071 AN Amsterdam
conservatoriumhotel.com
+31 20 570 0000

The Dylan

At the prestigious Keizersgracht, through a quaint little courtyard and past a row of bikes for guest use, one enters the beautiful canal building that houses the Dylan. The décor is pared back and contemporary; there are forty unique rooms, with all the expected five-star features, and there is also a small, well-equipped gym. Vinkeles, its beautiful Michelin-starred restaurant, specialises in French cuisine. Booking weeks in advance is essential. For something extra special, intimate meals are served on the hotel's salon boat, or, for a more relaxed occasion, there is a tasteful courtyard where you can enjoy lunch, dinner or drinks. The hotel prides itself on its service, and excellent concierges are on hand for special requests or recommendations. All of this, combined with its location, a stone's throw from top attractions and designer shops, makes the Dylan the city centre's premiere boutique hotel.

€€€€

—

Keizersgracht 384, 1016 GB Amsterdam
dylanamsterdam.com
+31 20 530 2010

Generator
Hostel

€

In just twenty years, Generator Hostels have become the last word in cool but affordable accommodation, and this branch epitomises all the style and attention to detail that has made this a leading brand. It is located in an old university science building in the east of the city, and many of its rooms (ranging from double and quadruple rooms to a luxury apartment for six) offer terrific views of Oosterpark. The building has retained its unique academic atmosphere, with the lecture theatre now housing the bar and the library offering a place for relaxation. Like the best hostels, Generator celebrates the social opportunities of travelling, and its layout and events programme, which includes DJ nights and basement parties, make this a great place to meet new people.

—

Mauritskade 57, 1092 AD Amsterdam
generatorhostels.com/en/destinations/amsterdam
+31 20 708 5600

Hotel Seven One Seven

€€€€

Hotel Seven One Seven, with its prime location overlooking the stunning Prinsengracht, is as close as you can get to staying in a traditional Amsterdam canal house. It was the first boutique hotel of its kind in the Netherlands, and celebrated its twentieth year in 2017. The building is grand and old (the façade dates from 1810, the rear from the seventeenth-century), and the interior is suitably genteel. The nine rooms are large, tastefully decorated, and named in honour of creative geniuses; the two executive suites, Picasso and Schubert, also offer views of the canal. The hotel is very deliberate in its approach; a continental à la carte breakfast is served, and guests can enjoy afternoon tea, or glasses of house wine in the evening, while the excellent concierge service is always on hand to reserve any of the city's restaurants for dinner. While the hotel is traditional, all the usual modern expectations, including Wi-Fi, are also catered for. With an overall atmosphere of an elegant gentlemen's club, this is an authentic getaway for grownups.

—

Prinsengracht 717, 1017 JW Amsterdam
717hotel.nl
+31 20 427 0717

Hotel V Nesplein

Hotel V has three beautiful locations across Amsterdam, each combining classic design with modern Dutch touches. The four-star Hotel V Nesplein, located in the heart of the theatre district, is a marriage of luxe theatrical flourishes, tempered by 1930s tones, and cool industrial lines and textures. Every detail has been considered and it comes as little surprise to hear that the owner has a background in hotel interior design. There is a great restaurant on the ground floor, where you can enjoy a meal before heading out onto Dam Square for the evening. Also highly recommended are the company's other hotels, the 1970s-inspired Hotel V Fizeaustraat and Hotel V Frederiksplein, which also offers self-catering lofts.

€€€

—

Nes 49, 1012 KD Amsterdam
hotelvnesplein.nl
+31 20 662 3233

The Hoxton

The Hoxton brand originated in London's Shoreditch in 2006, and a quick
glance at its locations – including Paris and Williamsburg, NY – gives
a clear idea of the demographic: this is where the really cool people
go. The Hoxton Amsterdam has 111 rooms and the aesthetic is suitably
eclectic, with grey-infused blues and greens contrasted with dark wood,
brass and cool tile. Rooms range in size, from 'Shoebox' to 'Tubby' (the
latter can't be booked but can be requested, so be sure to try your luck),
and all have Wi-Fi and off-centre perks like an hour of free international
calls and a daily breakfast bag. The super Lotti's restaurant, with its
Italian–Dutch menu, has a retractable roof that is open in good weather,
and at night there is always a big crowd who flock here for exhibitions,
launch parties or just cocktails and people-watching.

€€

—

Herengracht 255, 1016 BJ Amsterdam
thehoxton.com/holland/amsterdam/hotels
+31 20 888 5555

Morgan & Mees

Hotelier Myrthe Slotemaker opened Morgan & Mees with her partners in 2015, inspired by the idea of travellers and locals mixing with one another. They refurbished this 1880s building, careful to preserve its charm, then added modern interiors, with a predominance of black, steep staircases and shining herringbone floors. The result is a contemporary boutique hotel that is suffused with character. There are nine elegant rooms, some with balconies, and treats like Marie-Stella-Maris toiletries (pg. 48). Downstairs, there is a bar and a restaurant serving a Mediterranean-inspired menu. Service is extremely friendly throughout, led by the helpful and hands-on Myrthe. Morgan & Mees' location in the vibrant Jordaan area, just a five-minute walk from the Anne Frank House, makes this the perfect base for discerning travellers who appreciate both refined surroundings and mingling with locals.

€€

Tweede Hugo de Grootstraat 2-6, 1052 LC Amsterdam
morganandmees.com
+31 20 233 4930

Pulitzer

The Pulitzer is set within twenty-five seventeenth- and eighteenth-
century canal houses, once part of the playground of traders and
aristocrats. These were renovated in 2016 and the hotel pays homage
to its heritage. The atmosphere is one of buzzing sophistication; the
interiors are dark and relaxing, and the network of buildings surrounds
a leafy garden with a terrace serviced by Pause café. Guests can
dine in Jansz restaurant, which treats classic cooking with reverence,
before retiring to the bar, which oozes Dutch elegance. The rooms
on offer include luxurious themed 'extraordinary suites', such as the
romantic Book Collector's suite, but all are unique and comfortable,
some with canal views and balconies. The hotel also has a 24-hour gym
and its own classic canal boat, offering guided tours to guests.

€€€

—

Prinsengracht 323, 1016 GZ Amsterdam
pulitzeramsterdam.com
+31 20 523 5235

Sir Albert Amsterdam

This imposing nineteenth-century edifice in the De Pijp area was
once a diamond factory; today, it's presented as the mansion of
the elusive fictional aristocrat Sir Albert Amsterdam, a building
that marries old-school grandeur with sultry modernity – imagine
if James Bond moved into the hotel game. This is a fun concept
realised in a cool and grown-up way. The ninety rooms, ranging
from the compact Sir Boutique to the Sir Albert Residence, are
all bright, stylish and well appointed. The restaurant, Isakaya, has
excellent Asian food and a wide-ranging bar, making it popular with
visitors and locals long into the evening. For the morning after, an
adjacent gym is accessible to guests, or bikes can be hired for those
who would prefer some fresh air in the Museumplein or Vondelpark.

€€€

–

Albert Cuypstraat 2-6, 1072 CT Amsterdam
siralberthotel.com
+31 20 305 3020

Stout & Co.

Stout & Co. is a guesthouse in a former 1960s brewery building, €€
in a quiet residential area approximately thirty minutes' walk from
Museumplein. The exterior is unassuming, but when you spot the open-
plan office you'll know you're in the right place: this is the interior design
and landscape architecture studio of the owners, who live on the top
floor. It is no surprise, then, that this is an immaculately designed space.
There are five spacious, airy rooms, each with its own kitchenette
and entrance. Concrete floors, crisp linens and carefully selected art,
magazines and greenery add to the sense of expertly curated comfort.
A continental breakfast – all organic, of course – can be enjoyed in the
minimalist dining room or on the terrace, encapsulating this winning
combination of cool design hotel and intimate bed & breakfast.

—

Hoogte Kadijk 71, 1018 BE Amsterdam
stout-co.com
+31 20 220 9071

W Amsterdam

The W Hotel is split across two buildings, a former bank and a telephone exchange, and this intriguing concept of duality continues throughout. This is no small feat when you consider its size, with 238 rooms and 28 suites, crowned on the Exchange side by a panoramic cocktail bar and outdoor rooftop pool. And yet every detail has been given clear consideration. There is a playful contrast of heritage and modernity in the cool interiors – even the stylish rooms are a blend of curves and razor-sharp lines. There are also two restaurants, the refined Duchess in the Bank building and the more muscular Mr Porter on the upper level of the Exchange. Both are recommended. With a spa, a vibrant night-time crowd, and an ever appealing calendar of 'happenings', a super chic and fun break is guaranteed at the W.

€€€

—

Spuistraat 175, 1012 VN Amsterdam
wamsterdam.com
+31 20 811 2500

Shops

Ace & Tate

Ace & Tate is an innovative indie brand based in Amsterdam that is swiftly changing the country's eyewear industry. By subverting the supply chain, Ace & Tate is making chic contemporary prescription glasses available at a fraction of the traditional price. By manufacturing their own designs they control costs, so you can update your look for a quarter of what you might pay elsewhere. The brand has a growing online presence, and two stores in Amsterdam, where this fuss-free, modern ethos is reflected in the interiors. The flagship, on Huidenstraat, has pale oak panelling with peg holes, allowing the displays to change quickly, and as you wait for your appointment in the testing room, with its grey woollen walls, you can peruse the latest independent magazines.

Huidenstraat 20HS, 1016 ES Amsterdam
aceandtate.nl
+31 20 214 9054

American Book Center

The American Book Center began life in 1972 as an edgy bargain bookstore, selling cheap books and adult magazines, and operating the same hours as the local sex shops. Today it is a bustling three-storey English-language bookshop and a pillar of the cultural community. It is an independent, family-run business that prides itself on its passionate staff and extensive catalogue. Even considering its size, the selection here is remarkably broad, with a strong art section and an excellent range of international papers and the coolest magazines. The perfect place to buy something to read for the journey home, you are likely to lose track of time browsing the shelves of the ABC.

—

Spui 12, 1012 XA Amsterdam
abc.nl
+31 20 625 5537

Anna + Nina

Anna de Lanoy Meijer and Nina Poot started their company in 2012, and today they have three gorgeous Amsterdam stores specialising in unique covetable but affordable pieces from their own line and from other interesting brands. Their style is eclectic with global influences, and the stores include jewellery, accessories, decorative homewares, stationery, and a small clothing line (we love the beautiful silk pyjamas and kimonos), much of it sourced from India and Indonesia. There is something special to suit every budget, so this is the ideal place to treat yourself to a little reminder of your trip to Amsterdam.

—

Kloveniersburgwal 44, 1012 CW Amsterdam
anna-nina.nl/en
+31 20 261 1767

Baskèts

Founded in Amsterdam in 2012, menswear brand
Baskèts combines the best of street culture
and ready-to-wear fashion. The stores are very
cool, minimalist and industrial in style, much like
the pieces on sale, which are unified by clean
simplicity. Labels include Adidas, Obey, Saucony
and Baskèts originals, and the hottest new lines
are always to be found in store. This is masculine
streetwear with swagger and finesse; don't be
surprised to find scented candles, premium
skincare and high-end shoe-maintenance kits
alongside the sneakers and apparel.

—

Elandsgracht 57-59, 1016 TN Amsterdam; Gerard Doustraat 96, 1072 VX Amsterdam
baskets-store.com
+31 20 428 4071; +31 20 470 1010

De Bijenkorf

From its humble beginnings as a small haberdashery shop in 1870, de Bijenkorf has grown into a retail institution, with seven luxury department stores nationwide, the flagship of which looms over Dam Square. The building is an Amsterdam icon, housing five immaculate floors of the world's premium brands across fashion, beauty, homewares and gifts. In addition there is a spacious modern restaurant, an art gallery, talking-point window displays, and a calendar of stylish events. Whether you are looking for something special or simply some aspirational window shopping, de Bijenkorf will cater to all your luxury needs.

—

Dam 1, 1012 JS Amsterdam
debijenkorf.nl/amsterdam
+31 800 0818

Concerto

Spanning five shopfronts on the quaint shopping street of Utrechtsestraat, music shop Concerto opened its doors in 1955 and has boasted a dedicated fan base ever since. The shop sells an astonishingly wide range of new and second-hand CDs, DVDs, and vinyl, and needless to say music aficionados can, and do, spend hours flicking through its racks every day. All genres are represented, each with its own resident expert who can advise on new releases or rare gems in stock. Alongside physical music, Concerto sells concert tickets and a growing range of headphones, turntables and accessories. Instore gigs are frequent and free; check the website for listings and time your visit to this Amsterdam institution accordingly.

—

Utrechtsestraat 52-60, 1017 VP Amsterdam
concerto.amsterdam
+31 20 261 2610

Concrete Matter

Concrete Matter is an enticing gift shop geared to all things alpha male. It was established by three creative friends as an online store in 2012, and its popularity saw it transition to bricks and mortar the following year. The shop's focus is on 'useful, durable and beautiful products', and this warm, atmospheric space has a fascinating range of accessories, tools, grooming products and so-called 'mantiques' – everything to suit the outdoorsman of refined tastes. The selection of high-end brands and unique curios is perfect for those of vintage sensibilities, so if you are in the market for beard oil, a limited edition axe, or a stuffed and mounted goldfinch, Concrete Matter should be your first port of call.

—

Haarlemmerdijk 127, 1013 KE Amsterdam
concrete-matter.com
+31 20 261 0933

Hôtel Droog

Established in 1993, conceptual design collective Droog is one of the country's most highly regarded brands, bringing together independent creatives to facilitate projects, events, and routes to market. Hôtel Droog is a unique space that plays with the conventions of the traditional hotel, inverting our expectations. At the very top of the three-storey seventeenth-century building is 'The One and Only Bedroom', where visitors can spend the night. Below this is an impressive exhibition space, a café and events space, a fairy-tale garden, interesting indie concessions, and, of course, the beautiful Droog shop, where you can buy furniture, smaller design objects, books and apparel. Every element of this inspiring building has been carefully considered to reflect the Droog manifesto to 'create a dialogue between design and society'.

—

Staalstraat 7B, 1011 JJ Amsterdam
droog.com
+31 20 523 5059

Hutspot

Hutspot is a chic concept department store, spanning 800 square metres over two floors. On the ground floor there is a wide range of interesting brands for men, women and the home, and ethical fabrics and manufacturing are to the fore. There is also a stylish barbershop, where men can take five or refresh their look before shopping. Upstairs is a lunchroom, serving breakfast, sandwiches and salads, and a gallery space, which often hosts events like launches and workshops. A self-styled 'curator for an urbanised lifestyle', Hutspot began as a pop-up, but the owners created such a cool, cosy atmosphere in which to browse for unique pieces and up-and-coming talent that it is now a permanent space, and another branch has opened at Rozengracht 204.

—

Van Woustraat 4, 1073LL Amsterdam
hutspotamsterdam.com
+31 20 223 1331

Marie-Stella-Maris

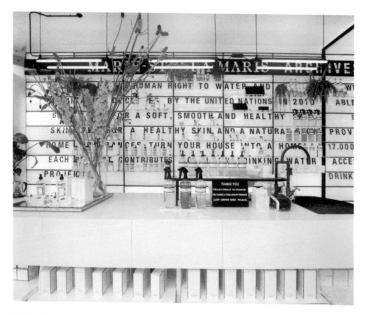

Marie-Stella-Maris is a refreshing shopping experience in every way. The brand was founded in Amsterdam by Patrick Munsters and Carel Neuberg in response to the 2010 UN declaration on the Human Right to Water and Sanitation. With every purchase of the company's natural care products and mineral water, a donation is made to clean-drinking-water projects around the world. Their products are available in a number of countries, but this flagship is the brand's only dedicated shop, and it is a beauty. Bright and shining, the monochrome interior is subtly punctuated by plants, and a cinema light-box wall showcases its 100 products to wonderful effect. Downstairs, there is a little bar that serves coffee and mineral water at weekends.

—

Keizersgracht 357, 1016 EJ Amsterdam
marie-stella-maris.com
+31 85 273 2845

Mendo

Mendo's founders describe it as a 'candy store for book aficionados', and this is some seriously well-selected, high-end candy. The shop was established in 2002, with three definite principles: to offer an impeccable selection of creative books, to provide a personal bookselling service, and to have a stunning shop design. Specialising in architecture, interior, fashion, photography and graphic design titles, it's an inspiring collection, and browsing is enhanced by the beautiful space. The walls are lined with thousands of black Mendo books that can be removed and rearranged to make space for other titles, creating a fluid and chic layout. A trip to this taste-making shop is a must for book lovers, and you can get lost for hours discovering the very best in creative book publishing.

—

Berenstraat 11, 1016 GG Amsterdam
mendo.nl
+31 20 612 1216

Stach

Popular organic deli Stach has six locations dotted around the city, each on a corner, making them easy to spot and filling them with light. Inside the aesthetic is hip and shelves groan under the weight of tempting produce. Alongside groceries, Stach offers coffee, fresh bread, and inventive seasonal take-out meals, like carpaccio and truffle mayo sandwiches, and lobster chips with chilli. Most stores are compact, but the Jordaan premises has a number of tables, where you can sit and watch the world go by. The Nieuwe Hoogstraat Stach has a winning location; it has a slim seated mezzanine but we recommend that you order to take away and sit along the beautiful canal outside. The friendly staff will help you to find everything you need for a delicious, healthy picnic.

—

Various
stach-food.nl

X BANK

X BANK is a unique concept store showcasing the best in art, design and fashion in an exhibition-style setting. Located in the Bank building of the W Hotel (pg. 32), it is part shop, part cultural centre dedicated to showcasing the work of local creatives (they currently stock over 180 different Dutch brands). On entering the early-twentieth-century building, you are met with a cool gallery space displaying contemporary art, and a white winding staircase brings you to the main shop floor, which is teeming with beautiful objects. Everything from haute couture to books to flowers is available in the 700 square metre venue, which also has an inspiring calendar of events throughout the year. Connecting you with the best Dutch talent in a stunning environment makes X BANK a truly memorable shopping experience.

—

Spuistraat 172, 1012 VT Amsterdam
xbank.amsterdam
+31 20 811 3320

What
to See

A'DAM
Toren

Pay a visit to the observation deck of Amsterdam Tower to experience an amazing 360-degree panoramic view of the city. The busy port, canals, and the surrounding landscape look spectacular from this height. If you're feeling brave, try 'Over the Edge', a swing that sends you hurtling out over the edge of the building, 100 metres above the ground. While you are there, explore the interactive exhibition on Amsterdam's history and culture, and try the great restaurant and café.

—

Overhoeksplein 1, 1031 KS Amsterdam
adamtoren.nl
+31 20 237 6310

Anne Frank House

The building where Anne Frank, the thirteen-year-old Jewish wartime diarist, lived and then hid from Nazi oppression with her family, is now an extraordinary biographical museum. The original manuscript of Frank's diary, historical documents, photographs, and original objects that belonged to her family and others, bring the tragic events to life. Her horrific story, so well related in her diary, is a hugely significant part of Second World War history and thus her house is a place of massive importance. Unsurprisingly the queues can wrap around the block, so book in advance.

—

Prinsengracht 263-267, 1016 GV Amsterdam
annefrank.org
+31 20 556 7105

Begijnhof

The peaceful sanctuary of Begijnhof feels worlds away from the bustle of Amsterdam city centre. The enclosed courtyard dates from the fourteenth century, and the buildings that surround it were formerly occupied by the Begijntjes, a sisterhood of unmarried Catholic women who lived together as a community. The last member of the Begijntjes died in 1971, but the buildings still house single women, and there is a long waiting list to rent here. To the south of the courtyard is the English Reformed church, which dates from the fifteenth century, and still has its original tower. Visit for a relaxing break from the sounds of the city.

—

Gedempte Begijnensloot, 1012 RM Amsterdam
begijnhofamsterdam.nl
+31 20 622 1918

Blijburg aan Zee

In hot weather, do as the locals do and get on a tram to the beach club at Blijburg. It is located on the man-made island of IJBurg, on the outskirts of Amsterdam. The beach is calm and relaxing, with pale sand and people playing volleyball, lazing about in the water and generally enjoying themselves. The beach restaurant has an exotic vibe and surprisingly good food, including tapas, pizzas, burgers and salads. At night, the party really gets started, with live music, DJs playing until 4am, bonfires, and themed parties. In the winter, the café is cosy and a lovely place to hang out.

Pampuslaan 501, 1087 LA Amsterdam
blijburg.nl
+31 20 416 0330

The Nine Streets

Known affectionately as the De Negen Straatjes or 'the nine little streets', this is a quirky area of vintage and designer shops, bars, restaurants, galleries and cafés. Located in the old town, it's made up of nine cobbled streets, bordered by the Leidsegracht on the south and Raadhuisstraat on the north. The area dates from the seventeenth century, when the canals were dug out around the medieval town centre. These days it's the place to come for cool cafés, fashion boutiques and second-hand bargains.

—

de9straatjes.nl/en/home

De Pijp

The bohemian area of De Pijp could be classed as Amsterdam's 'Latin Quarter', brimming as it is with trendy terrace cafés, shops, bars and international restaurants. It's also home to the beautiful landscaped gardens of Sarphatipark and to the famed Albert Cuyp Market (pg. 112), which is surrounded by over one hundred shops. It was originally built in the nineteenth century as housing for the working classes of the city. These days, the long narrow streets of the area are popular with artists and students of all different cultures, and the relaxed cosmopolitan vibe makes it a great place to spend an afternoon.

—

Rijksmuseum

Located on Museum Square, the Rijksmuseum is one of the most famous museums in the world. It has been open since 1800, and in its current building (designed by Pierre Cuypers) since 1885. Its focus is on both history and art, and as you might expect from the Dutch state museum, the art collection is quite magnificent, boasting works by Vermeer, Rembrandt and van Dyck. A modern extension was added in April 2013, and today the glorious Rijksmuseum is an unmissable Amsterdam attraction. Buy your tickets in advance so you can skip the queues.

—

Museumstraat 1, 1071 XX Amsterdam
rijksmuseum.nl
+31 20 674 7000

Stedelijk Museum

The Stedelijk Museum is known affectionately as
'The Bathtub', owing to the shape and smooth white
surface of the new wing, which was added in 2012.
The original building dates from the nineteenth century
and was designed by Adriaan Willem Weissman. This
impressive international museum houses modern and
contemporary art and design; among the many stars
of the art collection are works by van Gogh, Kandinsky,
Cézanne, de Koonig, Matisse, Chagall and Pollock. The
fascinating design collection looks at design from the
1900s up to the present day, and features furniture,
ceramics and jewellery.

—

Museumplein 10, 1071 DJ Amsterdam
stedelijk.nl
+31 20 573 2911

Restau-
rants

Bordewijk

This excellent restaurant is located next to the Noordermarkt in the Jordaan neighbourhood (look out for the tiny sign outside). Behind its many windows, which look out onto the market, the contemporary interior includes chic black seats and ultra-modern strip lighting. The menu, however, is definitely classic French – expect lobster, veal and game – and uses locally sourced products. Try the daily tasting menu and choose from their excellent selection of wines.

€€€€

—

Noordermarkt 7, 1015 MV Amsterdam
bordewijk.nl
+31 20 624 3899

Brut de Mer

Brut de Mer is the place to go for fresh oysters and champagne in the uber-trendy De Pijp area. While oysters are definitely the speciality, they take all their seafood seriously here, so if oysters aren't your thing, there are plenty of alternatives to sample, including scallops and lobster rolls. It's a hip and elegant little spot with friendly and obliging staff; the waiters here really know what they are talking about when it comes to shellfish. If you're lucky, you'll nab a seat outside.

€€

—

Gerard Douplein 8II, 1072 VE
brutdemer.nl
+31 20 471 4099

Buffet van Odette

Buffet van Odette is a bustling and chic restaurant café. The benches and tables on the outdoor terrace offer views of the canal and a great atmosphere, while the interior is inviting and cosy in colder weather. The food is healthy and hearty, and mostly organic. It's great at any time of the day but it is especially popular for breakfast and lunch. Breakfast is a simple affair, with croissants and other pastries, and at lunchtime, the abundant buffet is available, with a range of deliciously fresh salads, soups and quiches to choose from.

€

—

Prinsengracht 598, 1017 KS Amsterdam
buffet-amsterdam.nl
+31 20 423 6034

Café George

Café George is part of a group of excellent Dutch restaurants, and the inspiration here is 'a French brasserie in New York ... but in Amsterdam'. The menu includes all the classics you would expect from a French brasserie, such as seafood and steak frites, but you can also choose pastas and pizzas. The tiled walls and trendy furnishings lend the space a modern but relaxed vibe, and there is a fantastic outdoor seating area. Try the blackened tuna.

€€

—

Leidsegracht 84, 1016 CR Amsterdam
cafegeorge.nl
+31 020 626 0802

De Kas

€€€€

In the beautiful Frankendael Park you will find the foodie haven of De Kas located in an old greenhouse that has been transformed into an elegant restaurant. As you might expect from the unusual location, much of the food is prepared using vegetables, herbs and edible flowers that come from the restaurant's own garden and nursery. The Mediterranean menu changes daily, and the beautifully presented plates are served on tables of crisp white linen. If the weather is forgiving, you can enjoy your meal or a glass of wine from their extensive wine list in the garden outside. Highly recommended.

—

Prinses Irenestraat 19, 1077 WT Amsterdam
restaurantas.nl/uk
+31 20 644 0100

De Luwte

De Luwte is the perfect destination for a romantic meal. If you're fortunate, you can grab a window table and enjoy the views of Leliegracht canal, but sitting at any of the restaurant's candlelit tables is a treat. The concise menu is Mediterranean with a Dutch twist, and each dish is carefully crafted, innovative, and beautifully presented. Try the Black Angus tomahawk steak for two and one of the amazing cocktails.

€€€

—

Leliegracht 26-28, 1015 DG Amsterdam
restaurantdeluwte.nl
+31 20 625 8548

Envy

Envy offers high-end food in a chic, informal setting. It is the place to go if you fancy sampling a wide variety of foods, as they specialise in small plates, both hot and cold, with seasonal delights such as oysters, game and interesting charcuterie. Watch the chefs work their magic in the open kitchen, as you enjoy the relaxed ambience in the dark, sexy dining room, with its seductive low lighting. If you are with a group, order a few plates each to share, or otherwise go for the tasting menu.

€€

—

Prinsengracht 381, 1016 HL Amsterdam
envy.nl
+31 20 344 6407

Gebr. Hartering

Gebr. Hartering (Brothers Hartering) is a small canal-side eatery, which has quickly established itself as one of the best restaurants in Amsterdam. And it is easy to see why. The timber interiors make for an intimate and unpretentious space, and a pleasant, romantic atmosphere. The Hartering brothers specialise in nose-to-tail dining, so you can expect some unusual cuts of meat to be on offer. There is a daily six-course menu from which you can sample the best farm-to-table produce from local suppliers, and indulge in the excellent wine they suggest with each course. Try the huge slow-cooked ribs or the beef grilled on charcoal.

€€€€

—

Peperstraat 10, 1011 TL Amsterdam
gebr-hartering.nl
+31 20 421 0699

Pllek

The best thing about Pllek is its setting. A quick twenty-minute ferry trip from Central Station will take you to the once-industral, now hip cultural mecca of Amsterdam Noord. Fashioned from shipping containers and complete with a man-made gravel 'beach', Pllek is the ultimate symbol of this up-and-coming district. The restaurant's atmosphere is electric, with a relaxed alternative crowd (including lots of students who live in the area) who come to enjoy the views of the IJ River. The organic menu offers sandwiches, salads, and fresh juices at lunchtime, and a more adventurous dinner selection, including great seafood and vegetarian options. It gets fun and lively in the evening, so be careful not to miss the last ferry back.

€€

—

Tt. Neveritaweg 59, 1033 WB Amsterdam
pllek.nl
+31 20 290 0020

Restaurant As

Restaurant As is considered by many locals to be the best restaurant in Amsterdam. Its home is an odd-looking building, which is in fact a former church that was designed by Lau Peters, in the financial district of the city on the edge of Beatrixpark. Using produce sourced from local suppliers, the chef, Sander Overeinder, takes international cuisine and gives it a distinctly Dutch flavour. The menu changes by the day, reflecting the seasons and the weather, and uses age-old cooking methods such as pickling, curing and smoking. The sourdough bread alone makes it worth the visit.

€€€

—

Prinses Irenestraat 19, 1077 WT Amsterdam
restaurantas.nl/uk
+31 20 644 0100

Rijsel

Rijsel is the Flemish word for the city of Lille, and, as you might guess, the food here is inspired by French–Flemish cuisine. Located in a former domestic-science school, the setting is pared back, industrial chic, with bright lights, school-canteen-like chairs, and an open kitchen. There are usually tempting chickens turning on rotisserie skewers in sight of the diners. The ethos is no-nonsense, good-quality, reasonably priced food in a relaxed atmosphere. Booking ahead is necessary.

—

€€€

Marcusstraat 52, 1091 TK Amsterdam
rijsel.com
+31 20 463 2142

Ron Gastrobar

In 2013, chef Ron Blaauw announced that he would be closing his double-Michelin-starred restaurant, and opening a more inclusive, affordable and relaxed establishment in the same location. Thus, Ron Gastrobar was born. The menu does not differentiate between starters and mains; instead all the dishes are roughly the same size, with a flat price for all, and they are perfect for sharing. The dining room is smart and elegant, with a large heated outdoor area. The new venture has already been awarded a Michelin star, but it remains, as promised, a wonderful place to sample haute cuisine without the associated stuffiness or high price tag. Choose the ribs or the steak tartare.

€€€

—

Sophialaan 55 hs, 1075 BP Amsterdam
rongastrobar.nl
+31 20 496 1943

The Fat Dog

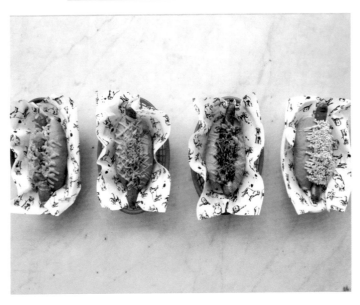

At the Fat Dog, Michelin-starred chef Ron Blaauw
takes the ultimate street-food staple, the hot dog,
to the next level. This is high-concept fast food: hot
dogs with exotic toppings like foie gras are served
in retro utilitarian baskets, and washed down with
champagne and cocktails in a cool, no-nonsense
space. By taking this basic dish, refining it and
experimenting with unexpected accompaniments,
Blaauw has created a dining experience that
is very cheap, really cheerful and extremely
satisfying. Try the Casablanca – lamb sausage
with baba ghanoush, caraway cucumber and spicy
mayonnaise.

€

—

Ruysdaelkade 251, 1072 AX Amsterdam
thefatdog.nl
+31 20 221 6249

The Harbour Club Kitchen

The Harbour Club Kitchen is a short taxi ride away from the city centre, in an area known as the Old South and within the four-star Wyndnam Apollo Hotel. It is beautifully situated on the waterfront where the five Amsterdam canals meet, and from the spacious terrace you can observe the boats pulling up as their occupants come to eat. If this all sounds terribly relaxing, don't be fooled, as the Harbour Club Kitchen has a serious party atmosphere, with DJs everywhere you look, even in the bathroom. The crowd is glamorous and the interiors are suitably funky, with large booth seats and eye-popping graffiti on the walls. Enjoy the fresh sushi and high-quality meats and seafood.

€€€

—

Apollolaan 2, 1077 BA Amsterdam
theharbourclub.com/kitchen
+31 20 570 5731

Toscanini

Toscanini is the top Italian restaurant in Amsterdam, specialising in authentic cuisine from the south of the country. Set in a beautiful old building, the dining room is large and elegant, with the open kitchen lending the space a touch of drama. It is well known that the key to excellent Italian food is simplicity and purity of the ingredients, and Toscanini subscribes to this ethos, placing a lot of emphasis on the provenance of their food (they work with many small farmers and slow-food producers in Italy). The wine list is strictly Italian only, which is a great way to discover new, interesting varieties. Toscanini is very popular with locals, so booking is essential.

€€

—

Lindengracht 75, 1015 KD Amsterdam
restauranttoscanini.nl
+31 20 623 2813

Worst
Wijncafé

€

'Wine-and-sausage café' Worst is reknowned for its nose-to-tail cooking, and more specifically the variety of sausages (think lobster or wild boar varieties), preserved meats, and patés, much of it made in-house. Despite its tiny size, it has a huge reputation amongst Amsterdammers. It is adorned with big and small tables and stools, and from the benches lining the outside window, you can watch the world go by as you sip on one of the excellent wines; there are over two hundred varieties on the list.

—

Barentszstraat 171, 1013 LC Amsterdam
deworst.nl
+31 20 625 6167

Cafés

Bar Spek

After a heavy night on the town, get on your bike and head to Bar Spek to nurse your hangover and satiate your bacon cravings. This is the best kind of neighbourhood café, with cool vintage-inspired interiors and a nice mix of locals, families and in-the-know tourists. There's a great breakfast menu, and soups, sandwiches and pizzettas for lunch (with vegetarians well catered for). One of the star dishes is the Spek Plank, a cured meat board with salami, prosciutto, and marinated bacon. When you've recovered, come back for one of the café's Gin & Tonic Friday events, where you can enjoy one of its famously generous measures on the broad terrace overlooking the canal.

—

Admiraal de Ruijterweg 1, 1057 Amsterdam
barspek.nl
+31 20 618 8102

Bocca Coffee

Amsterdammers take their coffee very seriously, and Bocca is a contender for the best in the city. The café's interior is simple, bright and airy, with light wood and splashes of greenery, and the coffee is exceptional. Bocca is owned by the Simons brothers, Menno and Tewis; they have been working with coffee for over fifteen years, and theirs was the first Dutch company to manage the entire process, from selecting the best beans to importing them and selling them to the public. They started the café to connect with their customers directly, and they have come in their droves to sample blends from Ethiopia, Colombia, Brazil, Indonesia and Kenya, bought directly from farmers.

—

Kerkstraat 96, 1017GP Amsterdam
bocca.nl
+31 32 131 4667

CT Coffee & Coconuts

CT Coffee & Coconuts offers a drink called the 'Harry Nilsson' (fresh young coconut with lime on the side – and a shot of dark rum if you're feeling adventurous), and this encapsulates the laid-back, retro Californian vibe of this café. Located in a 1920s building that was once the Ceintuur Theater, it's a huge space over four levels and it is always a hive of activity. They serve very high-quality single-origin coffee, and grind beans on demand for customers who want to bring a taste of Coffee & Coconuts home. The breakfasts and bites are delicious, and the extensive evening menu has a global feel, with Korean, Thai and Middle Eastern influences, complemented with wines and craft beers.

—

Ceintuurbaan 282-284, 1072 LR Amsterdam
ctamsterdam.nl
+31 20 354 1104

Gartine

This tiny charming café, nestled away on a back lane off a busy shopping street, is definitely worth seeking out. A proponent of the slow-food movement, Gartine operates a mature garden that supplies the kitchen with fruit, vegetables and herbs. The freshness of the ingredients and the dedication of the team are evident on every plate. They serve delicious breakfasts, lunches, cakes, and a more elaborate range of afternoon teas, perfect for a special occasion. The décor, with eclectic antique crockery and a Portuguese chandelier, is just the right side of quirky, and while it is bijou, this is a hugely popular spot, so advance booking is advised.

—

Taksteeg 7, 1012 PB Amsterdam
gartine.nl
+31 20 320 4132

Lot Sixty One

Lot Sixty One is a small but perfectly formed corner café whose size belies its significance as one of the city's top coffee roasters. The décor is cool, with white tile, distressed furniture and rough-hewn wood, and a few steps down from the bar area is the heart of the operation, the colossal Probat coffee roaster that is really worth seeing. Seating on this level tends to get hot when the machine is working, so try to get a seat on one of the benches outside. There is usually a meandering line of locals and connoisseurs from further afield waiting for the acclaimed coffee, so it's definitely worth a trip, perhaps *en route* to the nearby Foodhallen market.

—

Kinkerstraat 112, 1053 ED Amsterdam
lotsixtyonecoffee.com
+31 61 605 4227

Rum Baba

Rum Baba is a hip little café that isn't afraid to show a bit of personality. The quintessential corner frontage, pale wood and exposed lights are jolted onto the next level by the electric-blue floor and the clever murals on the walls by artist Tom Kraanen. The coffees, loose-leaf teas and pastries are exemplary (the banana bread is a particular hit), and you can also get more substantial breakfasts or toasties. Only five minutes from Oosterpark, Rum Baba balances serious coffee with a friendly demeanour; it's a relaxing place for a sightseeing break, to read, or to catch up on work, and you're sure to come away with a spring in your step.

—

Pretoriusstraat 33, 1092 EX Amsterdam
rumbaba.nl
+31 20 846 9498

Winkel 43

Beloved by tourists and locals, Winkel 43 is famous city-wide for its celebrated apple pie. Situated on a beautiful square by the Noorderkerk, the café serves interesting lunch and dinner menus (dishes include game broth with smoked duck, and salmon cannelloni) but most flock here for the apple pie. Homemade every day, it is somewhere between a traditional tart and an apple cake, rustic and wholesome, with coarsely chopped apple and served in generous warm portions with whipped cream. The top-secret recipe has been passed down between owners since the 1980s. Winkel is also a great place for a coffee or a drink, especially on the terrace, which is pleasant in summer or winter, and particularly on Saturday mornings, when the adjacent organic farmers' market (pg. 116) makes Winkel busy but buzzing.

—

Noordermark 43, 1015 NA Amsterdam
winkel43.nl
+31 20 623 0223

Bars & Clubs

Bar Bukowski

Named after the cult American writer Charles Bukowski, this attractive little bar features quotes from the author on the walls and on the menu. It is quite famous amongst Amsterdammers, and once a month it holds packed literature nights that always feature readings of Bukowski. The lower lever has a bar and a dancefloor, while the upper level is often the stage for a live band. There is definitely a buzz to this place and it attracts a fun group of people. There is a great selection of beers to choose from, and breakfast and lunch are also available. Sample the Dutch staple bitterballen with your beer.

—

Oosterpark 10, AE 1092 Amsterdam
barbukowski.nl
+31 20 370 1685

Café Waldeck

The interiors are the highlight of Café Waldeck, incorporating, as they do, many of the design elements of a classic art deco Parisian bar, with brass accents, velvet seats, petrol-blue walls and a pink bar in the centre of the space. Soak up the ambience over lunch or dinner, or have a drink outside on the terrace. Later, it becomes a lively bar, staying open until 3am on Thursdays and Fridays. Café Waldeck is popular with locals, and known for its friendly staff and warm atmosphere.

—

Willemsparkweg 223, 1071 HC Amsterdam
cafewaldeck.nl
+31 20 723 5841

Door 74

The exclusive Door 74 is one of the most stylish bars in Amsterdam, and it enjoys a certain drama. You have to ring in advance to make a reservation, at which point you will be given the address, and behind its discreet black façade, the space has the feel of a prohibition-era speakeasy. With leather, dark wood, sultry lighting, and antique barware, this is a grown-up bar serving serious drinks, and the cocktails here are unrivalled in the city. A cool change of pace for a night on the town.

—

door-74.com
+31 6 3404 5122

GlouGlou

GlouGlou is a wine bar that successfully strikes that tricky balance between taking wine very seriously and taking itself too seriously. The atmosphere here is far from stuffy; there is a welcoming bistro feel, and the friendly staff know the list of organic wines inside out and are more than happy to advise. If you're hungry, you can order cheese platters and patés, served with crusty French bread, and if you find a wine you really like, pick up a bottle and bring it home. In the summer, opt for a seat outside on the sunny terrace.

—

Tweede van der Helststraat 3, 1073 AE Amsterdam
glouglou.nl
+31 20 233 8642

Hiding in Plain Sight

From the street, Hiding in Plain Sight might look just like the average Amsterdam bar. But when you enter, you will feel like you have been transported to the Roaring Twenties, with its antiques, chandeliers and vintage wallpaper. The bar serves cocktails exclusively, and a member of the staff, pristine in their fitted waistcoats, will courteously offer you water and free nibbles while you peruse the huge letterpress menu (try the house speciality, 'The Walking Dead'). There are a number of events throughout the week and live music on Thursdays. It gets busy at the weekend, so it's best to reserve a table.

—

Rapenburg 18, 1011 TX Amsterdam
hpsamsterdam.com
+31 62 529 3620

Jimmy Woo

Jimmy Woo is perhaps the most glamorous nightclub Amsterdam has to offer. With striking décor over two floors, there are Asian accents in the lounge area, with Japanese screen doors and washi paper, while downstairs, the ceiling above the dance floor is adorned with thousands of little lightbulbs that flash in patterns to the tempo of the music. Every night of the week has a different resident DJ offering an eclectic range of music, including soul and R&B. Be advised: they operate quite a strict and elusive door policy.

—

Korte Leidsedwarsstraat 18, 1017 RC Amsterdam
jimmywoo.com
+31 20 626 3150

Louis

There is a lovely neighbourhood-pub vibe in this idiosyncratic corner bar, and with the books and board games sitting on the shelves, you might feel like you have accidentally stumbled into someone's living room. The distinctive interior has wooden features with steel accents, and exposed brick walls. The menu includes a delicious range of wholesome sandwiches and other snacks, such as meatballs and nachos. In the summer, people pour out onto the street to enjoy the view of the canal. Try the braised beef sandwich with a local beer.

—

Singel 43, 1012 VC Amsterdam
louis-amsterdam.nl
+31 20 752 6328

Paradiso

Located near the Leidsplein – the centre of Amsterdam's bar and club scene – the world-famous Club Paradiso is situated in a converted nineteenth-century church. This site has long been associated with hippy counterculture, after squatters took over the building in 1967 in an attempt to transform it into a cultural centre. Today, the venue hosts some of the biggest names in club music, with Thursday nights being particularly popular. Aside from the nightclub, the venue has hosted many of the world's most famous bands over the years, including Nirvana, the Rolling Stones and Arcade Fire, and it also stages plays, fashion shows, and exhibitions.

—

Weteringschans 6-8, 1017 SG Amsterdam
paradiso.nl
+31 20 626 4521

Porem

Located close to the Nieuwmarkt, this cocktail bar takes its name from a Dutch slang word meaning 'face'. It's a dark and cosy little bar with no sign, so keep your eyes peeled for the doorbell, which you must ring for entry. It serves classic cocktails, with the emphasis on old favourites made well rather than passing fads, and also offers a range of Asian snacks (dim sum and sushi, amongst others). A night spent here is often a wild one.

—

Gelderskade 19, 1011 EJ Amsterdam
poremamsterdam.com
+31 62 261 4496

Roest

Roest – meaning 'rust' – is an unforgettable venue that is
as innovative and creative as you can get. The concept
was put together on a shoestring by an artistic collective,
who transformed a former shipyard into a café, bar,
city beach and event space. Along with the industrial
warehouse interior which hosts the café and bar, at the
man-made beach customers are invited to go for a dip in
the summer, or to eat lunch *al fresco*. In the large event
hall you can expect to find markets, film screenings, gigs,
and other events taking place. Experiencing Roest, in all its
creative industrial madness, is an amazing way to spend an
Amsterdam evening. DJs perform at the weekends.

—

Jacob Bontiusplaats, 1018 LL Amsterdam
amsterdamroest.nl
+31 20 308 0283

Supperclub

Supperclub is not for the faint-hearted. With pole dancing, singing, videos projected onto the white walls, and sushi being eaten straight off people's bodies, it's a place where anything can happen. From your table or your bed you can enjoy a five-course dinner, while enjoying the various performances that take place each night. After 11pm, the restaurant vibe gives way to that of a club; DJs begin and the party stays going until 5am. Whatever shape your evening takes, a night in Supperclub will definitely be a night to remember.

—

Singel 460, 1017 AW Amsterdam
supperclub.amsterdam/en
+31 20 344 6400

The Butcher

On the famous Albert Cuypstraat, the Butcher serves top-quality burgers in a bright, white-tiled space styled as a butcher's shop. But book ahead and you will be given an esoteric password that will allow you entry into one of the coolest cocktail bars in Amsterdam, that is situated behind a hidden door at the back of the room. The bar is entirely different to the burger bar, with a dark and sultry vibe. The bar staff know their cocktails and are happy to assist you with the dizzying drinks menu. Booking is essential.

—

Albert Cuypstraat 129, 1072 CS Amsterdam
the-butcher.com
+31 20 470 7875

Vesper

This tiny, dark cocktail bar in the Jordaan area has
a supremely intimate and laid-back atmosphere.
Named after James Bond's drink of choice, the
bar's extensive cocktail menu includes nods
to Bond, his girls and his enemies. There are
also plenty of great wines and beers to be had,
if mixed drinks aren't your thing. It's a really
cool place to go for an intimate evening, or to
unwind with one of their 'high-tea cocktails' after
shopping in the Noordermarkt. We recommend
that you try the signature Vesper Martini or the
Raspberry Mimosa.

—

Vinkenstraat 57, 1013 JM Amsterdam
vesperbar.nl
+31 68 724 4056

Markets

Albert Cuyp Market

With 260 vendors, the hundred-year-old Albert Cuyp street market is said to be the largest in Europe. Stretching along a kilometre in the dynamic De Pijp area, lucky locals come here for their fresh produce. The fish on offer is incredible, with numerous varieties of lobster, crab and oysters that often appear on the menus of the city's restaurants. Take time to peruse all the stalls before stopping at one of the food stands. Try two Amsterdam favourites: the traditional herring, which is an acquired taste, and the famous stroopwaffle, freshly made and smothered in caramel and chocolate sauce, which is sure to please everyone. If you can, visit later in the week, when the convivial atmosphere is at its best.

Monday to Saturday, 9am to 6pm.

—

Albert Cuypstraat, 1073 BD Amsterdam
albertcuyp-markt.amsterdam

Bloemenmarkt

The stalls of Amsterdam's flower market float on boats and platforms on the Singel canal, between the Leidseplein and Kalverstraat. It has been running since 1862, and while it does operate daily throughout the year, it is in summer that the market really shines. Depending on the time of year, you can purchase the fresh flowers or the bulbs and seeds, and vendors can advise on which products are fine to bring home. Located a short stroll from the main shopping area, it's a nice departure from the high street, and you can buy some seasonal souvenirs or have a bouquet made up for your hotel room.

Monday to Saturday, 9am to 5.30pm; Sunday, 11.30am to 5.30pm.

—

Singel 630 to 600, 1017 AZ Amsterdam

IJ-Hallen

IJ-Hallen is a flea market that takes place one weekend a month in two shipping warehouses in the NDSM Docklands (an area that is now a cultural hub). The cool industrial setting, the colossal ceilings of the building, and the scale of the market itself elevates the atmosphere above that of a typical flea market. With 750 stalls selling clothes, accessories, books, records, and furniture, this is a true treasure hunt. Vendors generally want to clear their stands, so there are real bargains to be had. Admission is €5 (€2 for children) and a stamp allows you to come and go, so if it coincides with your visit, take the free ferry from Central Station, spend a few hours exploring, and then head to Pllek (pg. 75) for lunch.

Saturday and Sunday, 9am to 4.30pm. Check the website for dates.

—

Tt. Neveritaweg 15, 1033 WB Amsterdam
ijhallen.nl/en
+31 22 958 1598

Noordermarkt

Noordermarkt is the most popular Amsterdam market with locals, a fact reflected in its warm and friendly atmosphere. Located in the shadow of the seventeenth-century Noorderkerk on one of the city's prettiest leafy squares, it comprises an organic farmers' market and an antiques market. The origins of the antiques market date back to the seventeenth century, but today the twenty-year-old farmers' market is the more tempting part, specialising in unusual mushrooms and cheeses, alongside an impressive range of organic fruit, vegetables, meats, fish and freshly baked bread. There is a play park, and plenty of lunch options nearby, including the famous Winkel 43 café (pg. 93).

Saturday, 9am to 4pm (the antiques market is also open Monday, 9am to 2pm).

—

1015 DK Amsterdam

Waterlooplein Flea Market

As the oldest flea market in the Netherlands, the outdoor Waterlooplein Flea Market has an amazing history. Established in 1893 as a Jewish market, it played a commercially and culturally important role until the devastation of World War II. In the aftermath of the war, the market underwent a slow but steady renaissance, and in the 1960s and '70s it became a linchpin of youth culture, which it remains to this day. There are around 300 stalls selling vintage clothes, accessories, books and counterculture curios like military uniforms and graffiti spray paint. There are also a number of food stalls, offering cheap and cheerful dishes, located around the market.

Monday to Saturday, 9.30am to 6pm.

—

Waterlooplein 2, 1011 NZ Amsterdam
waterlooplein.amsterdam/en

Parks

Amsterdam Forest

A mere twenty minutes on the tram from the city centre, Amsterdam Forest is entirely man-made, and is three times the size of New York's Central Park. Do like Amsterdammers, and come here for respite from urban life: take a stroll through the woods, try the huge range of cafés and places to eat, take in the stunning views, and enjoy a performance at the open-air theatre. For the more active visitor, there is swimming, kayaking, fishing, cycling and more. It's an especially great day out if you have children in tow, with a petting zoo and pedal boats to rent. Camping and hotel accommodation is available for overnighters.

Open daily, 24 hours.

—

Bosbaanweg 5, 1182 DB Amstelveen
amsterdamsebos.nl/english/
+31 20 545 6100

Hortus Botanicus

The Hortus Botanicus Gardens are among the oldest
botanical gardens in the world, dating from 1638. They
were created as a herb garden to supply Amsterdam's
doctors and pharmacists, because a plague epidemic
was wreaking havoc. They are located close to the city
centre, and offer an especially enjoyable break from
the town in nice weather. Explore the lush greenhouse,
try the pleasant café with its large terrace, and view
the 6,000 species of indigenous and non-native trees
and plants. Don't miss the Butterfly Greenhouse.

*Open daily, 10am to 5pm (7pm on Sundays in July
and August).*

—

Plantage Middenlaan 2a, 1018 DD Amsterdam
dehortus.nl
+31 20 625 9021

Vondelpark

Located centrally, close to the museum quarter, the idyllic Vondelpark is where Amsterdammers go to jog, cycle, rollerblade, and picnic on the grass. With large English-style gardens, a teahouse, lawns and ponds, it receives an impressive 10 million visitors each year. The park is named after the poet Joost van den Vondel, of whom there is a bronze statue. If you're lucky, there will be a free concert playing when you visit. Look out for the open-air theatre and the statue entitled 'Fish', by Pablo Picasso.

Open daily, 24 hours.

—

hetvondelpark.net

Westerpark

Near the city centre, in the bustling Westerpark neighbourhood, you well find the expansive public park that give the area its name. The park offers a pleasant atmosphere, with locals cycling and jogging; rest assured, however, with cute restaurants dotted around, a jazz café, a cinema, and a bakery, there is lots to do if you simply want to unwind. Look out for the nearby Westergasfabriek, a former gasworks which is now an important cultural hub. If you're in town on the first Sunday of the month, the park hosts a great market, full of creative, handmade pieces.

Open daily, 24 hours.

—

1014 Amsterdam

Check
What's
On

EYE Film Museum
Foam
Melkweg
Ziggo Dome

EYE
Film
Museum

EYE Film Institute Netherlands moved to its stunning new home, designed by Delugan Meissl, in 2012. It was the first cultural institution to relocate to the up-and-coming IJ Harbour area, and the impressive white building is suitably cool, inside and out. Hop on the free ferry at Central Station and you'll be there in just five minutes, ready to explore. Inside there are four cinema screens showing an incredible selection of movies, a film laboratory, an exhibition space, a great shop, and a very nice, relaxed café restaurant, which has an outdoor terrace with beautiful views across the water. For adults, cinema screenings cost €10 (cards only) and entrance to exhibitions is €12.50, but visiting the rest of the museum is free.

—

IJpromenade 1, 1031 KT Amsterdam
eyefilm.nl/en
+31 20 589 1400

Foam

Foam is a hugely influential arts organisation that champions photography, and its small but perfectly formed museum has a solid reputation for excellent exhibitions and for drawing big names. The museum is located in a narrow, hundred-and-fifty-year-old canal building, and its intimate but bright interior, highlighted by chrome and glass, is well designed to ensure that the photography is shown in the best possible way. Exhibits feature new and established artists from around the world; they change every two to four months, but there is always something exciting to view, whatever your prior knowledge of photography. General admission is €10, and after viewing the exhibits you can visit the bookshop, the library of photo books, and the basement café.

—

Keizersgracht 609, 1017 DS Amsterdam
foam.org
+31 20 551 6500

Melkweg

Melkweg (meaning 'Milky Way') is a great club and cultural venue housed in an old milk-bottle factory on the Amsterdam canal ring. It was founded in 1970 as a non-profit arts organisation, and the space has grown to comprise two concert halls, a cinema, a theatre and an exhibition area. It offers a diverse array of events, from performance art to regular club nights, and it draws big names from the Dutch and international music scenes. A wide variety of musical tastes are catered for, drawing an estimated 400,000 visitors per year. Opening hours vary (R&B Saturdays generally run from midnight to 5am), so check the website for current listings. Melkweg is a safe bet for an unforgettable night out, so don't miss this Amsterdam icon.

—

Lijnbaansgracht 234A, 1017 PH Amsterdam
melkweg.nl/en
+31 20 531 8181

Ziggo Dome

Ziggo Dome is the place to be when big-name acts come to Amsterdam, with diverse draws like Drake, Neil Young, Louis C.K., and Cirque du Soleil performing there recently. As with any arena of this scale, it is best for big sounds and big production values: at a full-capacity concert the atmosphere is electric. One newspaper affectionately termed Ziggo Dome 'Las Vegas on the Amstel', and there is definitely a great party vibe. The design has been well thought out, to offer clear views of the stage and great acoustics, and there are plenty of bars and lockers so you can let your hair down uninhibited by your valuables. Check the listings in advance of your visit.

—

De Passage 100, 1101 AX Amsterdam
ziggodome.nl/en
+31 900 235 3663

Before you visit Amsterdam, you might want to check out these books and films to give you a better sense of the city.

Books

Amsterdam
Ian McEwan

Awarded the Booker Prize in 1998, *Amsterdam* tells the story of old friends Clive and Vernon, a composer and a newspaper editor both at complex stages of their careers, who meet at the funeral of a mutual friend and one-time lover. Together they contemplate death and enter into a euthanasia pact that rapidly unravels their friendship and leads both men to dark, dangerous places. Their shocking actions eventually bring them to Amsterdam, where the denouement of this gripping study of mortality and morality plays out, and only one can prevail.

The Diary of a Young Girl
Anne Frank

The diary of Anne Frank needs little introduction, but it is truly required reading. The book is comprised of the writings of a thirteen-year-old Jewish girl whose family were forced into hiding in a secret annex at Prinsengracht 263 in Amsterdam during the Nazi occupation in 1942. The family managed to stay there undiscovered for two years, before they were found and deported, first to Westerbork concentration camp, and then to Aushwitz. Anne, then fifteen, and her sister Margot died of typhus in Bergen-Belsen concentration camp in spring 1945. Their father Otto, the only surviving member of the family, had a book of Anne's diaries published in 1947, and it is a work of incomparable impact and importance.

The Dinner
Herman Koch

In this tense novel, our unreliable narrator Paul Loman and his wife Claire arrive at an upmarket Amsterdam restaurant to dine with Paul's brother Serge, a politician of national importance, and his wife Babette. This elegant occasion is in fact something of a crisis summit; they are here to discuss an appalling crime committed by their sons. The complex characters and increasingly dark plot will keep you enthralled, as the cracks in their solid, sophisticated façades begin to show. With overtones of ink-black humour, some critics have suggested that *The Dinner* is a critique of Dutch manners and privilege.

The Fall
Albert Camus

Jean-Paul Sartre declared that *The Fall*, Camus's final work of fiction, was 'perhaps the most beautiful and the least understood' of the philosopher's books. It is set in Amsterdam, and most of the action takes place in a bar, where, over several drink-fuelled evenings, the tormented Jean-Baptiste Clamence tells a stranger the story of his life. It is told in a series of monologues that are dripping with regret, self-loathing and bitterness; once a successful Parisian lawyer, he has fallen from grace and is now condemned to life in Amsterdam. From its opening pages the city plays an important, atmospheric role in the story.

Films

Cheech & Chong: Still Smokin
(1983)

Comics Tommy Chong and Richard 'Cheech' Marin built their careers on a mutual appreciation for cannabis, so when they decided to set their fifth and final feature film in Europe, where else could they choose but Amsterdam? The film was conceived as a way to present their live material

in movie form; in the first half, Cheech and Chong are invited to Amsterdam to attend a fictional film festival in honour of Dolly Parton and Burt Reynolds, and the second half features their stand-up sequence. Filmed entirely on location, *Still Smokin* is a celebration of Cheech and Chong's signature stoner comedy.

Diamonds are Forever
(1971)

Never far from the centre of the action, and with a famous fondness for fashionable locations, James Bond arrives in an Amsterdam still flourishing from the cultural revolution of the 1960s. On a mission that takes him around the world, Bond is tasked with smashing a diamond-smuggling ring with a very sinister objective, directed by his nemesis Blofield. The scenes in Amsterdam are shot against a backdrop of canals and distinctive architecture; an entertaining primer for a visit to the city, it will get you in the mood for a cocktail at Vesper (pg. 109).

The Fault in Our Stars
(2014)

This tear-jerker, based on the John Green novel

beloved by millions of romantic teenagers the world over, tells the story of two young American cancer patients, Hazel and Augustus. When they meet at a support group a quiet romance blossoms, and a mutual love of literature brings them to Amsterdam, where they seek out Peter Van Houten, the mysterious author of Hazel's favourite book. Fervent fans of *The Fault in Our Stars* can often be spotted paying homage at the film's various locations around the city.

Turkish Delight
(1973)

Directed by Paul Verhoeven and starring Rutger Hauer, *Turkish Delight* was a massive success in the Netherlands, so it's surprising that it is not better known internationally. It is based on a novel by Jan Wolkers, and tells the tumultuous story of sculptor Eric and his lover Olga. The drama is bleak but rewarding, and Amsterdam shines throughout. *Turkish Delight* is roundly lauded by critics: it was nominated for the Academy Award for Best Foreign Language Film in 1973, and in 1999 it was named Best Dutch Film of the Century.

Check out these sites and accounts for the most up-do-date events and insights into Amsterdam life:

Influencers

Amsterdamian
amsterdamian.com

A rich and individual photo blog by an Amsterdam-based photographer showing the people and hidden corners of the city, through the four seasons.

By Sam
bysam.nl

An up-to-the-minute rundown of the hottest new eateries in town, written by a very serious foodie called Sam, who has a keen interest in Asian and healthy cuisine.

Chapter Friday
chapterfriday.com

A good-looking style and career blog that uses the Amsterdam streets as a backdrop.

Cravings in Amsterdam
cravingsinamsterdam.com

A mouthwatering food blog interspersed with reviews of hot new Amsterdam eateries, spas and hotels.

I Amsterdam
iamsterdam.com

A useful guide for daily Amsterdam news and cultural events, with an online restaurant booking feature.

Mrs Mokum
mrsmokum.com

A very cool platform that celebrates all the talented artists, musicians, entrepreneurs, writers, designers, and creatives in the city.

Stuff Dutch People Like
stuffdutchpeoplelike.com

An amusing guide to the idiosyncrasies of the Dutch, that has spawned four successful books and developed a community of almost half a million followers.

Your Little Black Book
yourlittleblackbook.me

Anne de Buck's influential and aesthetically pleasing blog on all things Amsterdam, helpfully organised by neighbourhood.

Tips from the inside: we asked some top Amsterdam creatives for their favourite spots

Contributors

Maartje Diepstraten
bartsboekje.com

Maartje Diepstraten has been writing for magazines on the subjects of travel, food and drink, for almost a decade. She also operates bartsboekje.com, an extremely stylish Dutch-language website that focuses on these passions. She lives in the Jordaan ('Amsterdam's nicest area'), with her husband and her pug, Willem.

'How can I choose a favourite restaurant when it changes every week? Restaurant Breda (breda-amsterdam.com) is one of my ultimate faves. Anyone that you will ask will say Rijsel (pg. 77), and it is terrific, but my current preference is Scheepskameel (scheepskameel.nl), which is from the same owners. And Hotel de Goudfazant (hoteldegoudfazant.nl) in Amsterdam Noord. And Tales and Spirits (talesandspirits.com) in the city centre. I could just go on and on!

'I'm not that much of a clubber, but the views from Bar Ma'dam (madamamsterdam. nl) in the Sir Adam Hotel in A'DAM Toren (pg. 54) are amazing. My favourite cocktail bar is Vesper (pg. 109), which is close to my home in the Jordaan.

'I love Rika (rikastudios.com) and in par-

ticular Maison Rika (rikastudios.com/maison), which is their beautiful guesthouse with two rooms, just across from the store.

'Otherwise, I suggest an evening in Amsterdam's East Side: start at Bar Botanique (barbotanique.nl) and continue eating and drinking until you've reached Bar Basquiat (barbasquiat.nl).'

Nicole Huisman
@nicole_huisman

Amsterdam-based stylist Nicole Huisman made her name working with A-List companies such as *Glamour*, *Vogue* and Tommy Hilfiger, and was an *ELLE* stylist for five years. Nicole's acclaim as a stylist has won her a dedicated social media following of fashion addicts, who love her signature style.

'I visit Spaghetteria (spaghetteria-pastabar. nl/) at least once a week, because it's just around the corner (I live in De Pijp), it's cheap and it's always good. It's an easy-going Italian, with super friendly staff. I always eat the vongole – it's my true favourite. When I want to go for something fancier, I choose from the classics: Buffet van Odette (pg. 68), Wilde Zwijnen (wildezwijnen.com) and Red (restaurantred.nl). On Fridays, I like

ceviche and margaritas at Rosa's Cantina (rosescantina.com). I also like Toki (tokiho. amsterdam), where I go to work and to eat the best banana bread in Amsterdam, and GlouGlou (pg. 100) for extremely nice wines and olives.

'The Stedelijk Museum (pg.63) is, for sure, my favourite museum. The space is beautiful and the exhibitions mostly epic. I go to Zuiderziel (zuiderziel.nl) to shop for interior treasures, Mendo (pg. 49) for books, Neef Louis (neeflouis.nl) for furniture and props, and Wini (winivintage.nl) for the best vintage.'

Merel Kappelhoff
foam.org

Merel Kappelhoff is Head of Press & PR for Foam Fotografiemuseum Amsterdam (pg. 128). She came to the city to study, and now lives in Westerpark with her family. As Head or PR for Foam, she works on around twenty exhibitions per year, the acclaimed *Foam Magazine*, photography fair UNSEEN, and numerous educational projects.

'My favourite restaurant right now is Auberge Jean & Marie (aubergeamsterdam.nl/). It's quite new, and run by Dutch friends Jan and Marije, whose love for France and French cooking really shows. The food is amazing, with really high-quality ingredients skilfully cooked, and it avoids being pretentious. I love the no-nonsense, relaxed and comfortable atmosphere there, where the focus is on great food, fantastic wine and good company.

'Olives & More (olivesandmore.nl) is a lovely corner shop in the east of Amsterdam, which sells fifteen kinds of olives from more than ten countries. As the name would suggest, it also imports great olive oil, vinegars, artichoke hearts, sundried tomatoes, and other organic products. After years of working as a chef in Michelin kitchens, the owner Brian is an expert at turning all these fine products into the best tapenades, pestos and antipasti.

'Located in a former technical school building, De School (deschoolamsterdam.nl) is a bit out of the city, but it is worth the trip. It looks very industrial and rough from the outside, but it is amazing inside. The complex has a coffee bar, a restaurant, an art space and a club, as well as a gym, and a great terrace outside for barbeques in the summer.

'For culture, it is, of course, impossible to top Foam (foam.org) but I also love Ketelhuis (ketelhuis.nl), which is a fantastic arthouse film theatre situated in one of the buildings on the former industrial site of the Westergasfabriek (gas factory). It shows a terrific selection of films and documentaries and the location is beautiful. There are plenty of options for a beer after your film, on this spacious site in the middle of the Westerpark (pg. 123), and this is also where Foam hosts UNSEEN (unseenamsterdam. com) each September!'

Onno Kokmeijer
@kokmeijer

Onno Kokmeijer is a Michelin-star chef who, with Arjan Speelman, runs Ciel Bleu Restaurant on the 23rd floor of Hotel Okura Amsterdam (okura.nl). The view alone is worth the trip, but the two-Michelin-star food is very special, particularly at the chef's table, where you can watch Kokmeijer and Speelman at work.

'My favourite place to eat is the Michelin-starred Yamazato restaurant in Hotel

Okura Amsterdam. Their Japanese cuisine is excellent. Afterwards I might head to Supperclub (pg. 107), which is a very unique place at the Singel.

'If you're looking for culture, head to Theater Carre (carre.nl). It has a really nice atmosphere and very good shows. When I shop, I head straight for Shoebaloo (shoebaloo.nl) and Hugo Men (hugoboss.com/Nederland), although in general the Nine Streets (pg. 60) is a safe bet.'

Karin Swerink
vogue.nl

Karin Swerink is editor of the Dutch edition of *Vogue*. A journalist for over twenty years, she worked for a number of magazines before being asked to lead a Dutch version of *Glamour*, which was to become the largest fashion magazine in the country. She launched the first issue of Dutch *Vogue* in 2012, and regularly appears on television, most notably as a judge on *Holland's Next Top Model*.

'If you like to shop vintage, Salon Heleen Hulsman (salonheleenhulsmann.nl) has a great selection of second-hand designer clothes, shoes and accessories. You can find some truly unique pieces there (by appointment only). Another great boutique is Van Ravenstein (van-ravenstein.nl). It stocks beautiful garments by Dries Van Noten, Veronique Leroy, Junya Watanabe and A.F. Vandevorst, to name but a few. X BANK (pg. 51), a big store right in the centre of the city, has a comprehensive collection of mostly Dutch fashion, art and design.

'Foam (pg. 128) and Huis Marseille (huismarseille.nl) are two inspirational places to visit. Foam is a photography museum overlooking one of our many beautiful canals, and it shows a wide variety of international artists. Their bookshop may be small, but it has a carefully chosen selection of books and magazines. Huis Marseille is a photography museum as well, but it sets itself apart with its interesting choice of artists and it has an impressive permanent collection with a particular focus on contemporary Dutch, South African and Japanese work. As well as all that, the house itself is an old and majestic place, so it's definitely worth a visit.

'The Duchess (the-duchess.com) is a very nice and elegant place to dine; visit the tearoom or come for breakfast or lunch. The historic building in which it is situated is absolutely beautiful. For night-time, the brand new bar Ma'dam (madamamsterdam.nl) in the A'DAM Tower (pg. 54) is stunning. It is located on the twentieth floor, overlooking the water.'

Dennis Swiatkowski
dennisswiatkowski.com

Dennis Swiatkowski is a photographer who divides his time between Amsterdam and Cape Town. Aesthetically motivated by the hedonism and freedom of the past, his work often depicts nudity and nature as a gateway to an unreal reality created as a whole.

'The Otherist (otherist.com) is one of my favourite stores, as it stocks a plethora of unusual items, and, as an avid retro collector, I often walk in here to find contemporary and old curiosities to complement the other pieces in my apartment. De Negen Straatjes (pg. 60) is a cosy shopping area in the Amsterdam centre/Jordaan, which is host to a lot of smaller boutiques, and there are plenty of interesting stores to visit. For photography, I also really like Huis Marseille (huismarseille.nl) which showcases contemporary photography, and its building is majestic.

'The Stedelijk Museum (pg. 63) on the Museumplein houses some of the world's most inspiring contemporary arts pieces. Artists like Mondrian, Monet, Liechtenstein and others are on display, as well as new exhibitions every couple of months. Downstairs there is a space for experimental art, that shows mostly current and young artists. As a museum card holder, this place is one that I frequently visit to get inspired.

'Pompstation (pompstation.nu) is an excellent restaurant situated in the up-and-coming east side of Amsterdam. It's inside an old water pump station, and it serves the best steak. The dim lights and a smart interior plan give the place a great atmosphere and occasionally there are jazz nights, when guests can enjoy the music alongside their dinner and drinks.

'One of my favourite bars is Struik (facebook.com/cafestruik) on Rozengracht. It is not fancy – it's more of a locals' bar – and every month there is another artist showing his or her work on the walls. They also do Taco Tuesday, which is a personal favourite of mine, and it's where I usually meet my friends and see familiar faces.'

Francis van de Pavert
hellofrankie.com

Francis van de Pavert is the founder of Hello Frankie, a popular blog about design, style and travel, and owner of design company Hello Studio.

'Amsterdam is small, so it's the perfect city to explore by foot. I always advise people to visit different neighbourhoods, like the very popular De Pijp (pg. 61) but also De Baarsjes, a neighbourhood in the west of Amsterdam where you will find many independent stores like T.I.T.S. (tits-store. com), Misc (misc-store.com), De Balkonie (debalkonie.nl), and great places for lunch (Radijs, radijs-amsterdam.nl, Bar Spek, pg. 86) where you can mingle with the locals.

'One of my all-time favourite Amsterdam restaurants is Hotel Goudfazant (hoteldegoudfazant.nl). The location is industrial and the food is stunning. The best part is that you have to take the ferry to Amsterdam Noord, so for me the fun starts on the journey.

'Paradiso (paradiso.nl) is one of the most amazing clubs in Amsterdam because of its architecture (it is located in an old church), and the line-up is always interesting.

'KOKO Coffee & Design (ilovekoko.com) is one of my favourite places; it sells a mix of Scandinavian brands and Dutch design, and they also serve the best coffee. For kids, WijsWest (wijswest.nl) is just perfect, with its nice brands and cool gifts.'

Photography Credits

Pg.8 Pulitzer Hotel, Pg.13 Pulitzer Hotel, Pg.14 The Hoxton, Pg.16 Conservatorium, Amit Geron, Pg.17 Conservatorium, Amit Geron, Pg.18 The Dylan, Sander Baks, Pg.19 The Dylan, Roel Ruijs, Pg.20 The Generator, Nikolas Koenig, Pg.22 Hotel Seven One Seven, Pg.24 Hotel V Nesplein, Stefano Pinci, Pg.25 Hotel V Nesplein, Stefano Pinci, Pg.26 The Hoxton, Pg.27 The Hoxton, Pg.28 Morgan & Mees, Pg.29 Pulitzer Hotel, Pg.30 Sir Albert Amsterdam, Ewout Huibers, Pg.31 Stout & Co., Maarten Noordijk, Pg.32 W Hotel, Lutz Vorderwuelbecke, Pg.33 W Hotel, Lutz Vorderwuelbecke, Pg.34 Hôtel Droog, @ruu_da, Pg.36 Ace & Tate, Jordi Huisman, Pg.37 Ace & Tate, Jordi Huisman, Pg.38 American Book Center, Gerard van beek, Pg.39 Anna + Nina, Pg.40 Baskèts, Pg.41 De Bijenkorf, Pg.42 Concerto, Pg.43 Concrete Matter, Pg.44 Hôtel Droog, Thijs Wolzak, Pg.46 Hutspot, Pg.47 Hutspot, Pg.48 Marie-Stella-Maris, Pg.49 Mendo, Pg.50 Stach, Pg.51 X BANK, Patrick Bos Kessen, Pg.52 J.L. Marshall, Pg.54 A'DAM Toren, Pg.56 Getty Images/Photo 12/Contributor, Pg.57 Getty Images/Wilfried Wirth, Pg.58 Blijburg aan Zee, Dirk Kikstra, Pg.59 Blijburg aan Zee, Kimbely Muis, Pg.60 Getty Images/ Tim Graham/Contributor, Pg.61 Ger Bosma/Alamy Stock Photo, Pg.62 Rijksmuseum, Erik Smits, Pg.63 Stedelijk Museum, Pg.64 Café George, Pg.66 Bordewijk, Bob Bronshoff, Pg.67 Brut de Mer, Pg.68 Buffet van Odette, Moon Jansen, Pg.69 Café George, Pg.70 De Kas, Pg.72 De Luwte, Pg.73 Envy, William Maanders, Pg.74 Gebr. Hartering, Pg.75 Hemis/Alamy Stock Photo, Pg.76 Restaurant As, Pg.77 Rijsel, Janus van den Eijnden, Pg.78 Ron Gastrobar, Jorge Ferrari, Pg.79 The Fat Dog, Pg.80 Harbour Club Kitchen, Pg.81 Toscanini, Pg.82 Worst, Rene Mesman, Pg.84 Jasper de Waal, Pg.86 Bar Spek, Pg.87 Bocca Coffee, Jasper de Waal, Pg.88 CT Coffee & Coconuts, Pg.89 CT Coffee & Coconuts, Pg.90 Gartine, Pg.91 Lot Sixty One, Pg.92 Rum Baba, Pg.93 Peter Horree/Alamy Stock Photo, Pg.94 Wouter van der Sar, Pg.96 Bar Bukowski, Leon Hendrickx, Pg.98 Café Waldeck, Pg.99 Door 74, Eric Kleinberg, Pg.100 GlouGlou, Pg.101 Hiding in Plain Sight, Pg.102 Jimmy Woo, Pg.103 Louis, Pg.104 Paradiso, Joris Bruring, Pg.105 Porem, Pg.106 Roest, Pg.107 Supperclub, Wouter van der Sar, Pg.108 The Butcher, Pg.109 Vesper, Pg.110 shutterstock/arkanto, Pg.112 Horizons WWP/TRVL/Alamy Stock Photo, Pg.113 Paul Thompson Images/Alamy Stock Photo, Pg.114 IJ-Hallen, Nichon Glerum, Pg.116 Getty Images/Lucy Lambriex, Pg.117 robertharding/Alamy Stock Photo, Pg.118 Marijke Mooy, Pg.120 Marijke Mooy, Pg.121 shutterstock/Kitty Maguire, Pg.122 Getty Images/ Merten Snijders, Pg.123 Shutterstock/luismonteiro, Pg.124 Ernst van Deursen, Pg.126 Iwan Baan, Pg.128 FORGET Patrick/SAGAPHOTO.COM/Alamy Stock Photo, Pg.129 Foam, Christian van der Kooy, Pg.130 Milkweg, DigiDaan, Pg.131 Ziggo Dome, Pg.132 Shutterstock/S.Borisov